i

Profound Stuff

"The best stuff I've ever seen,
heard, read or said."

Larry Winget

Profound Stuff

Larry Winget
Copyright © MCMXCV

Printed in The United States Of America.

Cover and layout by Ad Graphics, Tulsa, Oklahoma.

Library of Congress Number: 95-161232

ISBN: 1-881342-08-5

Profound Stuff™ is a trademark of Win Publications!, Win Seminars!, and Larry Winget, denoting a series of products that may include but is not limited to books, pocket cards, calendars, audio cassettes and video tapes.

Published by:

Win Publications!

a subsidiary of Win Seminars! Inc.
P. O. Box 700485
Tulsa, Oklahoma 74170

To order more copies or to receive a complete catalog of Larry's personal development products, including information on his speaking services, call toll-free:

800 749-4597

Other books
by
Larry Winget

Dedication

To TRUTH.
Truth is everywhere; in every
circumstance, in every occurrence,
and in every individual. Help us to
recognize it and accept it in all of
its varied forms.

Introduction

Simply the best! That's what this book is. The best, most profound ideas and quotations that I have found in all of my reading and listening. I searched through over one thousand books and listened to over one thousand audio tapes to find what I consider to be the most profound thoughts regarding success at every level. These ideas transcend typical business philosophy and go beyond the cliches of the self help books. These ideas will help you uncover your true self, discover your purpose, return to a pure motivation of love, and exploit your uniqueness through the service of others. Read them over and over and take them deep into your heart and mind so they may help you achieve the level of life you were meant to experience.

Expect the best. Be prepared for the worst. Celebrate it all!

...Larry Winget

Live one day at a time. To worry over tomorrow's demands is to lose sight of today's blessings.

...Emmet Fox

*The person who sees
what he wants to see,
regardless of what appears,
will some day experience
in the outer what he has
so faithfully seen within.*

...Ernest Holmes

$\mathcal{I}$n one way or
another, you get what
you ask for in life.
$\mathcal{B}$e sure to ask for the
right things.

...Dick Sutphen

Discover your uniqueness and learn to exploit it in a way that serves others and you are guaranteed success, happiness, and prosperity.

...Larry Winget

Your outer world of
form and experience
is a reflection of your
inner world of
thoughts and feelings.
As above, so below.
As within, so without.
That is the Law.

...John Randolph Price

$\mathcal{W}$hatever we have
not let go of has
hold of us.

...Karen Goldman

Someday, after we have mastered the winds, the waves, the tides and gravity, we shall harness for God the energies of love. Then for the second time in the history of the world, man will have discovered fire.

...Teilhard de Chardin

When you end the
day, review and celebrate
your accomplishments,
sleep worry-free and wake
up enthusiastic about
creating another fulfilling
day.

...Dr. Jay Scott Neale

Service is the highest form of spirituality.

…Ramakrishna

We are bound by nothing except belief.

...*Ernest Holmes*

*Knowledge
is not power;
the implementation
of knowledge
is power.*

...*Larry Winget*

*The purpose of life
is to live in freedom
and joy and ease
until death moves
us on to whatever
comes next.*

...J. Kennedy Shultz

*Our own worst enemy
cannot harm us as much
as our unwise thoughts.
No one can help us as
much as our own
compassionate thoughts.*

...Jack Kornfield

*Your competitors
and enemies will
become your helpers when
you exult in their success.*

...Deepak Chopra, M.D.

*Success is being all
you can be in each area
of your life, without
sacrificing your ability to
be all you can be in each
and every other area of
your life.*

...Larry Winget

Laughter can add
more years to your life
than a step class.

…*Keds Advertisement*

Love and believe in what you do, the company you do it for, your customer, and yourself. This will not only bring you success, but happiness and satisfaction.

...Larry Winget

*The love we give away
is the only love we keep.*

...Elbert Hubbard

Your words, your product and your service are symbols of what you believe in and what you stand for.

...Larry Winget

$\mathcal{P}eace$ of mind occurs
when we put all our
attention into giving and
have no desire to get
anything from, or to
change, another person.

...*Gerald G. Jampolsky, M. D.*

Personal power comes from the strength of your choices and the steadiness of your belief in yourself.

...Jim Tunney

When you are afraid
of something you give it
the power to hurt you.

...*Larry Winget*

*According to your faith
let it be to you.*

...*Matthew 9:29*

*The size of your
success is determined by
the size of your belief.*

...Dr. David Schwartz

This moment is the
best moment of your life to
experience your illumined
self and to go forth and
express it.

...Frank Richelieu

*It's not what you are
that holds you back, it's
what you think you're not.*

...Denis Waitley

Fill your mind with the pure, the powerful, the positive, and the prosperous.

...Larry Winget

*In the presence of hope
. . . faith is born.
In the presence of faith . . .
love becomes a possibility.
In the presence of love . . .
miracles happen!*

...Dr. Robert Schuller

Happiness and love
are just a choice away.

...Leo Buscaglia

Your results have been determined by your beliefs. Change your beliefs and you will change your results.

...Larry Winget

*Happiness comes
when your work and
words are of benefit to
yourself and others.*

...Jack Kornfield

*You must see it first
in your mind if you
are ever going to see it
in your reality.*

...Larry Winget

*Faith is to believe
what we do not see; and
the reward of this faith is
to see what we believe.*

…St. Augustine

Beliefs generate your thoughts and emotions, which create your experiences. To change your life, change your beliefs.

...Dick Sutphen

*For by your words
you will be justified, and
by your words you will be
condemned.*

...*Matthew 12:37*

Your words are the outpicturing of your consciousness. If you want to know what you really believe, listen to your words. Nothing can change until your words change.

...Jack Boland

*If you lack any good
thing, you are still asleep
to your own good.*

...Florence Scovel Shinn

You can have just as much success and prosperity as you believe you deserve.

...Larry Winget

You are whole, complete, and your success in life will be in direct proportion to your ability to accept this truth about you.

...Dr. Robert Anthony

Implement now,
perfect later.

...*Larry Winget*

Let the one who is sad, depressed, or unhappy find some altruistic purpose into which he may pour his whole being and he will find a new inflow of life of which he has never dreamed.

...Ernest Holmes

*We find our happiness
not in solving all the
problems of the world, but
in ceasing to be one of
those problems.*

...J. Kennedy Shultz

Take a moment right now to appreciate yourself. You are unique. No one is exactly like you. No one has your talent, your ability, your aptitude, or your potential. No one can contribute exactly what you have to contribute. You are a Divine creation. Celebrate yourself!

...Larry Winget

*You were not put here
to make a living, but to
live your making and by
living your making, to
make your living.*

...Leo Brown

When we seek money, or a good relationship, or a great job, what we are really seeking is happiness. The mistake we make is not going for the happiness first. If we did, everything else would follow.

...Deepak Chopra, M. D.

Failure's most dangerous attribute is its subtlety.

...Jim Rohn

When you do for a man what he can and should do for himself, you do him a great disservice.

…Benjamin Franklin

*You can't build a
reputation on what you
are going to do.*

...Henry Ford

As you have done, it shall be done to you . . .

...Obadiah 1:15

*Do not forget little
kindnesses and do not
remember small faults.*

...Chinese Proverb

*What we call failure
is just a mechanism
through which we can
learn to do things right.*

...*Deepak Chopra, M. D.*

*When we become lax
in the expression of
gratitude, we become little
people with little minds,
leading little,
inconsequential lives.*

...Eric Butterworth

*If we just do what we
love, love what we do,
and express ourselves fully
and freely, we are serving
others in accordance to
our purpose. All that is
left is for us to open
ourselves to receive.*

…Arnold Patent

*Life is an opportunity
to contribute love
in your own way.*

...Bernie Siegel, M.D.

If any process or principle works at all, then it works for all.

...Larry Winget

The expression of gratitude is a powerful force that generates even more of what we have already received.

…Deepak Chopra, M. D.

*You are what you are
and where you are
because of what has gone
into your mind, and you
can change what you are
and where you are by
changing what goes into
your mind.*

…Zig Ziglar

We have only three basic needs: to belong, to be appreciated, and to be loved unconditionally. To belong, we must include. To be appreciated, we must first appreciate. To be loved unconditionally, we must love unconditionally.

…Pamela S. Carter

$\mathcal{W}$hatever is going on
is just a reflection of
ourselves back to us, so
that we can see ourselves
more clearly.

...*Arnold Patent*

$\mathcal{O}$ne of the basic laws
of human existence is:
find yourself,
know yourself,
be yourself.

...Dr. Norman Vincent Peale

Since love is our real purpose in life, and since it holds our universe together, you should exhibit love, harmony and cooperation in every action, and avoid showing anger, hatred and violence.

...Dr. Wayne Dyer

This time called life is
far more sacred and
special than any of us
could ever imagine. Our
task, or should I say
our privilege, is to become
more aware of the
specialness of life and to
participate in it as deeply
and as fully as we can.

...Tim Hansel

*What you say
about others says more
about you than it says
about them.*

...Larry Winget

$\mathcal{O}$ne of the most
important lessons that
experience teaches is that
on the whole success
depends more upon
character than either
intellect or fortune.

...William Lake

*There is no box made
by God nor us but that
the sides can be flattened
out and the top blown off
to make a dance floor on
which to celebrate life!*

…Kenneth Caraway

People will pay little attention to what you have to say. Most won't even believe what you have to say. However, they will pay attention to see if you believe what you have to say.

...Larry Winget

If you want something you have never had, you have to do something you have never done.

...Mike Murdock

We make a living by
what we get, but we make
a life by what we give.

...Winston Churchill

Many of life's failures are men who did not realize how close they were to success when they gave up.

...Thomas Edison

Each personality draws to itself personalities with consciousness of like frequency, or like weakness. Therefore, the world of an angry person is filled with angry people, the world of a greedy person is filled with greedy people, and a loving person lives in a world of loving people.

…Gary Zukav

We create our own reality. If our perception of reality is one of lack and limitation, then our reality will be lack and limitation. If we perceive the world to be a wonderful, loving, abundant, and exciting place, then that will be the kind of world we live in.

...Larry Winget

$\mathcal{A}$ guaranteed way to
avoid criticism:
Say nothing.
Do nothing.
Be nothing.

...*Unknown*

$\mathcal{W}$hen values are
clear, decision making
is easy.

...*Roy Disney*

$\mathcal{T}$he secret of living a
life of excellence is merely
a matter of thinking
thoughts of excellence.

…Charles Swindoll

The greatest good you
can do for another is not
just to share your riches,
but to reveal to him
his own.

…Benjamin Disraeli

$\mathcal{T}$he essence of genius
is knowing what to
overlook.

...*William James*

*Happiness may be
had only by helping
others to find it.*

…Napoleon Hill

Few people will turn to themselves to take responsibility for their results until they have exhausted all opportunities to blame someone else.

...Larry Winget

Peacefulness is the
door through which we
gain access to the
abundance of the
Universe.

...Arnold Patent

*If you inflict your
past wounds on the
present, you'll make your
future bleed.*

...Tom Hopkins

Love others as you would be loved, treasuring them as they are without expectations of change.

...*Dick Sutphen*

You can't afford not to be generous and giving of your time, efforts, talents, and money. Prosperity flows - open up the channels.

...Larry Winget

Goodness is the only investment that never fails.

...Thoreau

. . . you do not have
because you do not ask.

...James 4:2

When we hear
somebody complaining
that he has not enough,
we may know that he has
not expressed enough
appreciation for what he
already has.

...Lowell Fillmore

When you feel
grateful, you become
great, and eventually
attract great things.

...Plato's Law

*The measure of a man
is in the number of people
whom he serves.*

...Paul D. Moody

Whatever you vividly
imagine, ardently desire,
sincerely believe, and
enthusiastically act
upon will inevitably
come to pass.

...Paul J. Meyer

$\mathcal{A}$ forgiving attitude,
with its ability to open
hearts, is one of the most
loving gifts we can ever
give to ourselves.

...Arnold Patent

*Live every day
as if you were an
exclamation point.*

...Larry Winget

*You don't have to be
good to start, but you do
have to start to be good.*

…Unknown

You are a reflection of what you see, what you hear, and the people you associate with.

...Larry Winget

It is better to be prepared for an opportunity and not have one than to have an opportunity and not be prepared.

...Whitney Young

*After all is said
and done, more is said
than done.*

...Unknown

You cannot be totally committed sometimes.

> ...*A Course In Miracles*

*The more you are
thankful for what you
have, the more you will
have to be thankful for.*

...Zig Ziglar

*A rejected opportunity
to give is a lost
opportunity to receive.*

...Oral Roberts

*Everything you have
in your life is there
because you attracted it.*

...Mike Wickett

What you think about, talk about, and do something about, comes about.

...*Larry Winget*

Love all.
Serve all.

...Hard Rock Cafe

*Your rewards in life are
in direct proportion to
your service.*

...*Earl Nightingale*

*Success means we go
to sleep at night knowing
that our talents and
abilities were used in a
way that served others.*

...*Marianne Williamson*

Live long and prosper.

...The Vulcan Creed

Whatever you want,
wants you.

...Mark Victor Hansen

*First comes thought,
then organization of that
thought into ideas and
plans; then transformation
of those plans into reality.
The beginning, as you
will observe, is in your
imagination.*

...Napoleon Hill

$\mathcal{G}$uilt serves no purpose. There is no way to go back and change anything. Forgive yourself and move on.

...*Larry Winget*

A person acting from a motivation of contribution and service rises to such a level or moral authority, that worldly success is a natural result.

...Marianne Williamson

When we learn to
love another person, we
are really learning to love
a part of ourselves that we
previously rejected.

...*Arnold Patent*

*If you ask for success
and prepare for failure,
you will receive the thing
you have prepared for.*

...Florence Scovel Shinn

When we get
frightened, we want to
control everything, and
then we shut off the flow
of our good. Trust life.
Everything we need
is here for us.

...Louise Hay

What you resist you draw to you. As long as you resist something, you are locked into combating it, and you perpetuate its influence in your life.

...Dick Sutphen

With love and enthusiasm directed toward our work, what was once a chore and hardship now becomes a wonderful tool to develop, enrich, and nourish our lives.

...Jerry Gillies

Focus on a belief system of serving and loving others through your life, your love, your words, your product and service, and success and prosperity will be yours.

...Larry Winget

*It is useless to affirm
benefits, protection, supply,
guidance, and healing, if
all the time you are doing
things which you know are
not right in the sight of
God and man.*

...Catherine Ponder

Every choice has a consequence. By taking note of the consequences, we can decide to choose differently.

...Arnold Patent

When you have the choice between being right and kind, always choose kind.

...Wayne Dyer

*He who sows
sparingly will also reap
sparingly; and he who
sows bountifully will also
reap bountifully.*

...2 Corinthians 9:6

*We attract to us what
we first become.*

...Larry Winget

When you have finished your day, be done with it. Never save any of your load to carry on the morrow. You have done your best, and if some blunders and errors have crept in, forget them. Live this day and every day as if it all may end at sunset, and when your head hits the pillow, rest, knowing that you have done your best.

...Og Mandino

When one door closes,
another opens; but we
often look so long and so
regretfully upon the closed
door that we do not see
the one which has opened
for us.

...Alexander Graham Bell

Live neither in the past nor in the future, but let each day's work absorb all your interest, energy, and enthusiasm. The best preparation for tomorrow is to do today's work superbly well.

...Sir William Osler

As we have therefore opportunity, let us do good unto all men.

...Galations 6:10

*If you keep believing
what you've been
believing, then you'll keep
achieving what you've
been achieving.*

...Mark Victor Hansen

*Great things are done
by people who think great
thoughts and then go out
into the world to make
their dreams come true.*

...*Ernest Holmes*

Love is the law of God. You live that you may learn to love. You love that you may learn to live. No other lesson is required of man.

…Mikhail Naimy

Help ever,
hurt never.

...*The House Of Blues*

$\mathcal{I}$t is not easy to find
happiness in ourselves, and
it is not possible to find
it elsewhere.

...Agnes Repplier

*What lies behind us,
and what lies before us are
tiny matters, compared to
what lies within us.*

...Ralph Waldo Emerson

*Until we view
ourselves and what we do
as important and valuable,
no one else will.*

...Arnold Patent

$\mathcal{R}$*eal joy comes not from ease or riches or from the praise of men, but from doing something worthwhile.*

…Wilfred T. Grenfell

We can enrich our own lives, give to ourselves, and be as creative and happy as we will allow ourselves to be.

...Marlo Morgan

*Everything in life
gets better for us when we
get better, and nothing in
life gets better for us until
we get better.*

...*Larry Winget*

Success is the fulfillment of your uniqueness.

...*Eric Butterworth*

*What is easy to do is
also easy not to do.*

...Jim Rohn

We should expect the best and so live that the best may become a part of our experience.

…Ernest Holmes

*He who has found
the way of love will seek
no other.*

...Meister Eckhart

*Go first class
all the way and the
universe will respond by
giving you the best.*

...Deepak Chopra, M. D.

The only way to pass any test is to take the test. All tests on every level are always repeated one way or another until you pass.

...Marlo Morgan

There are no shortcuts
to any place worth going.

…Beverly Sills

We are here to make
another world.

...W. Edwards Deming

A man's true wealth is
the good he does in
the world.

...Mohammed

*When love and skill
work together, expect a
masterpiece.*

...*John Ruskin*

*A man is not finished
when he's defeated; he's
finished when he quits.*

...Richard Milhous Nixon

No one is coming to your rescue. It's all up to you. You have the power to change any condition.

...Larry Winget

$\mathcal{H}$elping others make money and helping other people to fulfill their desires is a sure way to ensure you'll make money for yourself as well as more easily fulfill your own dreams.

…Deepak Chopra, M. D.

Few men are lacking in capacity, but they fail because they are lacking in application.

...Calvin Coolidge

The nature of God is a circle of which the center is everywhere and the circumference is nowhere.

...*Empedocles*

The minute you begin to do what you want to do, it's really a different kind of life.

…Buckminster Fuller

In order for us to expand our capacity in any direction - mentally, physically, socially, economically - we need to connect with the spiritual nature of our being.

...Frank Richelieu

*Try then, today, to
begin to look on all things
with love, appreciation and
open-mindedness.*

...A Course In Miracles

In a realistic, here-and-now sense, my daily, moment-to-moment experience of God is to love and to serve and to give.

…Wayne Dyer

$\mathcal{L}$ove, compassion, and
tolerance are necessities,
not luxuries. $\mathcal{W}$ithout
them humanity cannot
survive.

...The Dalai Lama

$\mathcal{B}$etter is not something you wish; it's something you become.

...Jim Rohn

$\mathcal{C}$here is only one
thing stopping us from
having heaven on earth:
that we can't believe
it can be.

...Patricia Sun

*Life in abundance
comes only through
great love.*

...Elbert Hubbard

You can increase the flow of money, objects, and things you want into your life by operating with more clarity, joy, harmony, and integrity, trusting that what happens is for your higher good.

…*Sanaya Roman*

What you have done
to create where you are
can be undone and
redone to create where
you want to be.

...Larry Winget

*The secret of prosperity
is generosity, for by
sharing with others the
good that life gives us we
open up the well-springs of
abundance.*

...*J. Donald Walters*

*The thing you resist is
the thing you most
need to hear.*

...Dr. Robert Anthony

$\mathcal{W}$e are all born for
love. $\mathcal{I}$t is the principle
of existence, and its
only end.

…*Benjamin Disraeli*

*Where there is love
there is life.*

…Gandhi

The golden opportunity you are seeking is in yourself. It is not in your environment; it is not in luck or chance, or the help of others; it is in yourself alone.

...*Orison Swett Marden*

*You can have
everything in life you
want if you will just help
enough other people get
what they want.*

...*Zig Ziglar*

$\mathcal{G}$ood things come to
us so they can be used
by us in loving and
intelligent ways.

...Larry Winget

*You will have joy only
when you focus on
having it and settle for
nothing less.*

...Sanaya Roman

Work is love made visible....all work is emtpy save when there is love. And when you work with love you bind yourself to yourself, and to one another, and to *God*.

...*Kahlil Gibran*

*Go Big
or
Stay Home.*

...Larry Winget

Larry Winget

Larry Winget is an internationally recognized speaker and seminar leader. He is the author of more than a dozen books and the creator of many audio/video learning systems, as well as lots of other unique personal development products.

Known for his unique style, Larry's down-to-earth, humorous, bottom-line approach make his "stuff" fresh, fun, and easy to implement.

Larry is an active member of the National Speakers Association and a charter member of the Oklahoma Speakers Association. He speaks on the subjects of Success, Leadership, Teambuilding, Being Customer Obsessed, and Prosperity. He is also widely known as a humorist. Regardless of the topic, you can be assured that his material is centered on universal principles that will work for anyone, at any time, and in any business.

Larry believes that success in either our personal or professional life is not hard. It simply comes down to knowing what to do and doing it. He is committed to helping everyone understand that they deserve the best and can have it, when they follow a few simple principles.

Larry Winget has discovered his uniqueness and learned to exploit it by serving others. His symbol is the exclamation point. His heroes are Tarzan, Superman, and The Lone Ranger. His dogs are Elvis and Nixon. His wife is Rose Mary. His boys, Tyler and Patrick. His philosophy is, "Expect the best. Be prepared for the worst. Celebrate it all!"

For a complete catalog of Larry Winget's books, audio and video learning systems, and other unique personal development products, contact:

Win Seminars!
P. O. Box 700485
Tulsa, Oklahoma 74170
918 745-6606
800 749-4597